Young Heroes

Lindsey Williams
Gardening for Impoverished Families

Michelle E. Houle

KIDHAVEN PRESS
A part of Gale, Cengage Learning

GALE
CENGAGE Learning

Detroit • New York • San Francisco • New Haven, Conn • Waterville, Maine • London

GALE
CENGAGE Learning

© 2008 Gale, a part of Cengage Learning

For more information, contact:
KidHaven Press
27500 Drake Rd.
Farmington Hills, MI 48331-3535
Or you can visit our Internet site at gale.cengage.com

LIBRARY OF CONGRESS CATALOGING-IN-PUBLICATION DATA

Houle, Michelle E.
Lindsey Williams : gardening for impoverished families / by Michelle E. Houle.
    p. cm. — (Young heroes)
Includes bibliographical references and index.
ISBN 978-0-7377-3867-4 (hardcover)
1. Williams, Lindsey, 1987- 2. Food relief—United States—Citizen participation—Juvenile literature. 3. Young volunteers in social service—United States—Biography—Juvenile literature. 4. Social action—United States—Juvenile literature. 5. Gardening—United States—Juvenile literature. I. Title.
HV696.F6H674 2007
363.8'83092—dc22
[B]
                                                            2007022923

ISBN-10: 0-7377-3867-7

Printed in the United States of America
2 3 4 5 6 7 12 11 10 09 08

Contents

Food for the Hungry

Lindsey Williams experimented with tomatoes for eight years. She was trying to produce larger crops using fewer natural resources such as water. Her **innovations** include a growing technique that saves water while increasing crop yield. She also came up with a plastic irrigation piping system that uses metal rather than wood plant stakes. Lindsey encourages farmers to adopt her techniques in hopes of saving acres of trees and tens of thousands of gallons of water. Her discoveries have won many awards. As of March 2007, she has donated over 60,000 pounds (27,216kg) of produce to food banks that feed hungry families.

Throughout her life, Lindsey has worked for a variety of causes, such as environmental **conservation** and the fight against hunger. Along the way she has proven that girls have the power to excel in science and **philanthropy**.

Lindsey Williams found a way to grow more tomatoes using less water.

Lindsey has a long record of choosing causes important to her and taking action. The story of Lindsey Williams demonstrates that young people can make a difference in the world.

Chapter One

The Early Life of Lindsey Williams

Lindsey Williams, born on April 26, 1987, began to demonstrate her care and concern for others at a very early age. The child of several generations of farmers and gardeners, Lindsey was raised to believe that helping others is an important part of life. She learned these values from her sister, parents, and grandparents, all of whom placed a high value on activities such as volunteering.

During her childhood, Lindsey and her family lived in Faucett, Missouri, a small town in Buchanan County near the Kansas border. People in Faucett depend on family farms to feed and support themselves. Even if farming is not the main source of income for a family, many people earn extra money by growing large gardens and selling the surplus in driveways, roadside stands, and farmers' markets.

Lindsey's family was no exception. Her grandfather, a barbershop owner, had grown tomatoes ever since Lindsey's father was a young man. He would sell them from the back of his pickup truck. Growing tomatoes was a tradition in the Williams family. In fact, every year Lindsey's family had a contest to see who could grow the largest tomato by the Fourth of July.

Success or failure of farms in Buchanan County and elsewhere depends heavily on seasons, geography, and events of nature. The fact that Faucett is so close to the

Lindsey Williams grew up in Missouri farm country (pictured).

Missouri River, an important water source, is one reason that agriculture thrives in this area. But this closeness became a big problem when disaster struck in April 1993.

The Great Flood

Storms and wet weather that month greatly increased water levels in both the Mississippi River and the Missouri River. By the beginning of June, many **levees** along these rivers began to break, as continued rainfall raised water levels even higher. Still more heavy rain fell in July,

Although only six at the time, news of flooding in nearby farms and towns worried Lindsey.

to the point where river gauges designed to measure water levels broke or were **submerged.** By the end of the month, the Mississippi and Missouri rivers had swelled to nightmarish proportions, **displacing** people in Illinois, Iowa, Kansas, Minnesota, Nebraska, North Dakota, South Dakota, Wisconsin, and Missouri.

By August virtually all of the 700 levees along the Missouri River had been destroyed. But that was not all of the devastation that nearly 100 days of flooding brought to the people in its path. The Great Flood of 1993 had submerged 15 million acres (6.07 million ha) of farmland, destroyed approximately 10,000 homes, damaged 45,000 more, and killed 48 people. One of the towns affected by the flood was St. Joseph, which lies along the Missouri River about 16 miles (26km) north of Faucett. Scientists knew that the Missouri River would flood at St. Joseph if it grew deeper than 17 feet (5m)—and during the summer of 1993, the river peaked at 32 feet (9.75m).

A Need to Help

National, state, and local agencies rushed to help victims of the flood. The National Guard and Red Cross set up emergency shelters. Families who found themselves without basic essentials such as water, food, or a place to live turned to these shelters for assistance.

Television and newspaper coverage of the devastation inspired many people to take action. The Williams family was deeply affected by the images and stories of the families and children stranded and hungry. Although she was only six years old at the time, Lindsey clearly remembers thinking of the children who were staying in the shelters and had lost everything. She recalls, "I remember asking my dad if we could take some animals to the kids in the shelters."[1]

Lindsey's father, Jim Williams, had been an active community volunteer for years. He agreed to help her. "I asked if I could give some of my extra toys to the kids who lost theirs,"[2] she remembers.

Lindsey filled a large black garbage bag with stuffed animals and rode with her family to the shelter for the victims from St. Joseph. Distributing the toys to the children affected her greatly. Years later she recalled, "I still today remember the joyous feeling of helping those families."[3] It was a feeling that encouraged her to embark on a life of helping others in both small ways and bigger ones.

More Problems

The historic sights of St. Joseph, such as the Jesse James House and the Pony Express Museum, remained intact after the flood. But many important businesses did not survive. Inside one large manufacturing plant in the southern part of the city, water levels reached a depth of more than 4 feet (1.2m). The owners decided not to reopen. This meant that the company's 3,000 employees were now without a job. The economic strain on the displaced families increased as they had to deal with the additional burden of looking for work.

These hardships meant that more people than ever were having trouble feeding their families. Officials

A man clears debris from a flood-damaged store. Some stores never reopened.

with Missouri's Emergency Food Pantry System reported that most of the people using their services at this time were families with children and that many households had gone without food because of money problems.

11

This news was not lost on the Williams family, especially Lindsey. She knew that helping people had given her a good feeling. Her father suggested that food pantries were a great place to help. Lindsey remembered this five years later when she decided to grow her own garden.

Chapter Two

Scientific Experiments

In the fall of 1998, eleven-year-old Lindsey entered the sixth grade. That year, she learned something she had not realized before. She recalls, "We were reading about world hunger in class and how so many students go to school hungry. Our teacher told us that there was hunger right here in our own community and that the local food banks did not have enough food for everyone."[4]

Lindsey, who had always helped with her family's garden, decided that one way she could make a difference would be to grow her own garden to help feed the hungry. She planted 25 tomato plants in a plot of land and carefully tended her crop. She knew that the success of her plants would depend on the right combination of water, sunlight, and fertilizer. She had seen her father experiment with planting and remembered the different

Hoping to feed people in need, Lindsey grew 25 tomato plants.

methods he used. "My father would put special fertilizers on plants, they had to be planted on just the right moon sign, and the rows had to run a special direction,"[5] she said.

Lindsey wondered what she could change in the process to improve the outcome. She decided to conduct a science experiment in which she would test different brands of fertilizer to determine if one was better than another. To do this, she used one type of fertilizer on one group of plants and a different type on the rest.

A Successful Experiment

Much to Lindsey's delight, one part of her garden grew bigger and more numerous tomatoes. Her experiment a success, she decided to send her results to the company that produced the fertilizer. The company was pleased with her results and promised to send her supplies to conduct further experiments. Lindsey's father suggested that a food bank might be a good place for her to donate

Lindsey donated her tomatoes to a food bank like the one pictured here.

her tomatoes. Lindsey agreed. She contacted the food bank that served people in the Buchanan County area. Her father offered to drive the tomatoes there in his truck.

The people who worked at the food bank were happy to receive Lindsey's tomatoes. In 1998 emergency food pantries in Missouri gave out more food than they ever had before. Most of the hungry people they helped were families with children. Many of these families did not have enough money to buy food most of the time.

Not only did Lindsey donate the tomatoes from her own garden, she urged farmers in her area to do the same. She asked them to donate produce to a program she created called Gardening for Families. All the produce donated to the program helped people who received emergency food from the Central Missouri Food Bank Pantry.

Helping people with her tomatoes inspired Lindsey. She wondered if further experiments could produce even better results.

Sideways Planting

By early 2001 at the age of thirteen, Lindsey was spending her days studying alongside her eighth-grade classmates at Spring Garden Middle School. Her Gardening for Families program was helping fill the shelves at the food bank. And she was continuing the gardening experiments she had begun two years earlier.

Through her continued experimentation, Lindsey had made an important scientific breakthrough. In-

Traditional ways of planting do not work in places like this that suffer from drought.

stead of planting her plants the traditional way, in holes in the ground, she laid each plant sideways, in mounds of dirt. Lindsey called her method "open transverse planting." Although the plants are at first planted on their sides, sunlight raises the seedlings straight up within a matter of days. So, she notes, "You can't really tell that it's been planted differently until you dig the plant up and you realize that when you get down to the root system the roots are actually growing in an L-shape."[6]

Lindsey's planting technique was an improvement over the old way for several reasons. Because the roots were closer to the surface, water could reach them more easily. Lindsey knew that her discoveries could help people grow food in countries affected by **drought**. She explains: "What happens is, by the plant being planted transversely the roots are closer to the topsoil. So if you're having a drought, they're closer to the topsoil so they can take in more moisture because they're only about two to six inches deep, compared to if they're planted horizontally when they're anywhere between 14 to 20 inches deep."[7] Lindsey also found that because her plants could take in water more easily than those planted in the old way, they needed less water to grow. In addition, their roots grew bigger, and the tomato crops doubled.

A tomato seedling is planted in rocky soil.

Lindsey presented her results to the Missouri Junior Academy of Science in Joplin, Missouri. On April 20, 2001, the judges awarded Lindsey the Academy's Golden Eagle Award for her outstanding experiment. She told a newspaper reporter that she was shocked and excited to have won. And less than a week before her fourteenth birthday, Lindsey, already a prize-winning scientist and inventor, had yet another experiment planned.

Lindsey's Nutrient Delivery System

Every crop needs a watering system, so water delivery, also known as irrigation, became the subject of Lindsey's next experiments. She created an irrigation system made from plastic tubing that worked well with her open transverse planting method. Because crops require fertilizer in addition to water, Lindsey found a way to deliver both at the same time. She named her invention the Lindsey's Nutrient Delivery (LND) system.

The resulting water savings, increase in crop growth, and superior tomato production proved the success of the LND system. Lindsey wondered if the system would have the same effect on crops other than tomatoes. She tested it on zucchini and other squash and was thrilled when the results came up the same. Her successes with smaller vegetable crops inspired a hope that she would one day be able to test her system on large corn or soybean farms. As a result of all her experimentation, Lindsey had discovered a way to help feed people in her community and possibly help people around the world.

Chapter Three

Service and Recognition

By 2005 Lindsey, a senior in high school, had accomplished more than many adults. She had established the Gardening for Families food assistance program, invented both a planting technique and Lindsey's Nutrient Delivery system, and donated over 28,500 pounds (12,927kg) of produce to local food banks. She had come a long way since her first visit to a shelter twelve years earlier, where she had realized that helping people was very rewarding to her. And her accomplishments had consequences for people who lived far from her hometown of Faucett. In the areas of ecology, science, and the fight against hunger, Lindsey's experiments had helped people in real, measurable ways.

Ecological Benefits

Through her experimentation and environmental research, Lindsey had developed ways

to save water. This is important because farms throughout the world all require a tremendous amount of water, and water is a limited resource. The LND system re-
duces the amount of water used by 50 percent, while at
the same time increasing the output of the crops by as
much as 250 percent. So, the LND system is one way
that Lindsey promotes conservation.

Another technique that Lindsey uses and promotes
is the use of metal instead of wooden garden stakes.
Stakes are stick-like pointed objects placed in the
ground to support plants as they grow. Lindsey believes

A community garden provides fresh, homegrown produce for families in
need.

that thousands of trees would be saved every year if farmers and home gardeners switched their stakes from wood to metal.

According to Lindsey, her methods were copied successfully by large-scale growing operations nationally and internationally. Using her resourcefulness and creativity, she has combined her scientific skills with her desire to garden for families in need. She sums up her results this way:

> I started experimenting with fertilizer and then researched a special growing technique that doubled the amount of crops that grew. Then I made a special system that reduced irrigation water by over 320 billion gallons (over 1.2 trillion liters) a

Drip irrigation uses less water and gets the water where it needs to go.

year—that is the same amount of water as three major lakes! The system was made of plastic tubing that also replaced wooden garden stakes, saving over 58,000 trees annually. Every year I increased my garden plots, increasing my donations of fresh foods to needy families.[8]

Fighting Hunger

Between 1999 and 2003, the number of families without a dependable food source in the United States increased by 3 million households. Of these 3 million, 1.4 million were families with children. Yet many people are not aware that hunger is a problem for people in the United States. Because Lindsey knew about the problem and wanted to help, she was able to make a difference in the lives of hungry families. She noted in late 2005, "I've donated right at forty thousand pounds of fresh vegetables."[9]

Transporting that much produce is no easy task. Moving the food proved to be quite a challenge for Lindsey and her family. "We'll bring in an entire truckload of nothing but boxes of tomatoes, because you can't stack tomatoes on top of each other because they'll bruise," she says. "But when we bring in potatoes and green beans, there are five-gallon buckets in the back of my dad's Dodge Dakota."[10] Whether growing the food, harvesting the food, or hauling it somewhere, Lindsey was always involved. As a result, Lindsey's innovations and her accomplishments were beginning to attract attention.

Awards

The International Eco-Hero Award, sponsored by the organization Action for Nature, is awarded to young people between the ages of eight and sixteen. In 2004 the group chose Lindsey as one of nine Eco-Heroes of the year. The award, recognizing her efforts in ecology, came with a certificate and $75. This award was followed by many more.

In 2005 she won the Gloria Barron Prize for Young Heroes, and on February 17, the Missouri House of Representatives passed a resolution honoring her service and achievements. Later that year Lindsey graduated as the Mid-Buchanan High School Valedictorian for the class of 2005.

Also in 2005, Lindsey won the Prudential Spirit of Community Award. This award named her one of the top five youth volunteers in the United States. For this award she received a $5,000 college scholarship and $5,000 to spend as she wished. Always thinking of ways to help others, Lindsey donated half the money to an assistance program for girls. She gave the other half to 40 families in need during the Christmas holiday season.

Volunteers sort food delivered to food banks by the truckload.

On March 18, 2006, Lindsey was interviewed for *CNN Saturday Morning News*. In April she was recognized as one of *Teen People* magazine's 20 Teens Who Will Change the World! Also in 2006 she traveled to New York to join the first group of youths ever inducted into the National Kids Hall of Fame. Other awards she has received include the Intel Excellence in

DG   1000C.01

House Resolution No. 673

Whereas, from time to time the members of the Missouri House of Representatives pause to recognize the meritorious accomplishments of an exceptional Show-Me State student; and

Whereas, Lindsey Williams, a senior at Mid-Buchanan R-V High School, has achieved national recognition for exemplary volunteer service by receiving a 2005 Prudential Spirit of Community Award; and

Whereas, this prestigious award, presented by Prudential Financial in partnership with the National Association of Secondary School Principals, honors young volunteers across America who have demonstrated an extraordinary commitment to serving their communities; and

Whereas, the Prudential Spirit of Community Awards program is supported by the National 4-H Council, the Girl Scouts of the USA, the American Red Cross, the YMCA of the United States, the Points of Light Foundation, the American Association of School Administrators, the National Middle School Association, the National School Boards Association, the Council of the Great City Schools, the National School Public Relations Association, and many other national youth and service organizations; and

Whereas, the Prudential Spirit of Community Awards program is part of a broad initiative created by Prudential to encourage young people to become involved in community service; and

Whereas, Lindsey Williams earned this award by giving generously of her time and energy to plant and harvest garden vegetables to help needy families in her area for more than five years; and

Whereas, the success of the State of Missouri, the strength of our communities, and the overall vitality of American society depend, in great measure, upon the dedication of young people like Lindsey Williams who use their considerable talents and resources to serve others:

Now, therefore, be it resolved that we, the members of the Missouri House of Representatives, Ninety-third General Assembly, join unanimously in congratulating and honoring Lindsey Williams as a recipient of a Prudential Spirit of Community Award and in wishing her only the best in all future endeavors; and

Be it further resolved that the Chief Clerk of the Missouri House of Representatives be instructed to prepare a properly inscribed copy of this resolution for Lindsey Williams.

Offered by _____

Representative Martin T. Rucker
District No. 29

I, Rod Jetton, Speaker of the House of Representatives, Ninety-third General Assembly, First Regular Session, do certify that the above is a true and correct copy of House Resolution No. 673, adopted February 17, 2005.

Rod Jetton, Speaker

The Missouri House of Representatives passed a resolution (pictured) honoring work done by Lindsey Williams.

Environmental Science Award, the U.S. Air Force Outstanding Science Project Award, the U.S. Army Outstanding Science Project Award, and the Herbert Hoover Young Engineer Award.

Through it all, Lindsey remains modest. She says, "There are so many people out there doing the same thing I am, and they deserve just as much credit as I do."[11]

Chapter Four

Tools for the Future

After graduating from high school, Lindsey had to choose which college to attend. She traveled to Fayette, Missouri, to visit the campus of Central Methodist University. She says, "I thought, it's not too far from Columbia [Missouri], not too isolated. We headed to the heart of town and I said, 'This is awesome!' I looked around and thought, I really like it here."[12] After investigating the university's science program, she decided that Central Methodist University would be her school of choice. She entered as a freshman in the fall of 2005.

Her transition from high school to college has had some funny moments and has given her opportunities to talk about her accomplishments. She told a reporter from the *Kansas City Star*:

> Here, they bring in freshmen three days before upperclassmen. So we came in on

a Saturday for freshman orientation. One of the group activities was, we had this roll of toilet paper, and the group leader said, "We're going to be out in the woods for a week. Take as many pieces of toilet paper as you think you'll need to last the week." So the toilet paper's being passed around, and I notice the three advisers are taking, like,

Lindsey has become a role model for other young women interested in science.

five pieces each. I take three. Turned out we had
to tell one thing about ourselves for each piece we
had. This was before I found out I'd won the Barron Prize. So I said I graduated from Mid-
Buchanan High School; and my name's Lindsey;
and I've just been named one of the top five
youth volunteers in America. That was an award
from Prudential Financial. And after that, seri-
ously, I had four guys come up to me and want to
know what it was for. I was like, "Yes!"[13]

As a female student of science and **technology**, Lindsey has become a role model for girls who may have
avoided subjects traditionally considered masculine.
Lindsey, in her role as a dynamic, passionate young
woman scientist, has proven that girls have the ability
to succeed in science- and technology-related careers.

Girls in Science

The participation of girls in science is another cause
that Lindsey feels strongly about. Studies have shown
that when girls are in fourth grade they are just as interested in math and science as boys are. But by the
time they reach eighth grade, only half as many girls as
boys say that they find science and math interesting.

Lindsey hopes that this situation will change. She explains:

Science is a subject that has opened its doors now
more then ever to women. There are so many opportunities out there for anyone willing to work

for them. Science is a part of our everyday lives. When girls realize how much science affects them, they might find the joy in solving problems and carrying out experiments to test their own ideas and find answers to the questions they ask all the time.[14]

Personal computers, cell phones, and DVD and MP3 players are just a few examples of science and technology in everyday life. Advances in science affect nearly every aspect of modern life—from communication to entertainment to health and medicine. And science can be applied to the fight against hunger as well.

Fighting Hunger

According to the U.S. Department of Agriculture, in 2005, 11.7 percent of households in Missouri and 11.4 percent of households in the United States were either hungry or experiencing food insecurity. Food insecurity is the problem of not having daily access to food. Many factors contribute to food insecurity. For most families, the problem is a lack of money to buy food. For others, especially the elderly and people who live in rural areas, challenges include a lack of **accessibility** to a reliable food source.

In 2006 the Central Missouri Food Bank helped feed an astonishing number of people—more than 80,000 per month. This amounts to more than 20 million pounds (9.07 million kg) of food distributed to the elderly, the working poor, and other families in need. Food banks work through networks of agencies to assist

An agricultural engineer studies plant growth, something Lindsey Williams also hopes to do someday.

emergency food pantries, homeless shelters, low-income food programs, senior assistance programs, and other groups that serve people in need.

Lindsey's desire to pursue a career in the scientific field of **agricultural engineering** is another step in her journey to improve the accessibility of food for people in Missouri and around the world. Agricultural engineers research and develop systems that work with natural resources. They may design farm machinery, build flood control systems, and develop ways to conserve water and soil. Another area of study for some scientists in this field is food engineering. Food engineers may make structural changes in food, through science, to increase its nutritional value. Lindsey is hopeful that a career in agricultural engineering will enable her to discover new ways to improve the quality and quantity of foods that are grown in the future.

College Life

Lindsey enjoys a busy and active college life while she continues her studies. When she is not attending classes she spends her time working in the school laboratory and running track. She also works as a chemistry tutor, helping fellow students who are having trouble with the subject.

She says of her plans after college:

My plan is to attend graduate school. I want to pursue a masters or even a PhD in environmental chemistry. I really hope to someday work at a research facility. I want to work with agriculture or even conservation issues dealing with things from water conservation to testing waste run-off in streams. I love chemistry and I love the outdoors, so naturally the perfect career for me would bring those two things together.[15]

Chapter Five

Ways to Help

Lindsey Williams's commitment to helping people demonstrates that people of all ages can take action to improve problems in their community. Through her words and deeds, Lindsey brought about change in many areas. The interest in her enormous contribution of food to the hungry has inspired others to donate as well. The recognition of her scientific crop-growing innovations has led to more widespread use of her techniques. And the increased use of her methods has resulted in conservation of natural resources.

One common aspect of all Lindsey's successes has been her desire to solve problems. She says:

> I look at a problem and then decide what I can do to help eliminate it in my own community, similar to the hunger problem. I always look for practical, achievable solutions that have a positive impact. True, I was rewarded for my

volunteer efforts, but I worked harder at showing other people how important it is to become involved![16]

There are many different ways that people can get involved in solving problems such as food insecurity and conservation. Some ideas for bringing about change include growing community gardens and writing letters to elected officials.

Community Gardening

The problem of hunger exists in communities all across the United States. One tool that can help address this problem is the creation of a community garden. Community gardens are generally small plots of land owned

A community garden brings people together and provides healthy foods.

by groups of people or organizations. People work together to plant and cultivate the land into a source of beauty, pride, and sometimes edible produce.

Local park and recreation departments sponsor some community gardens, and others are renewal projects meant to clean up and beautify neglected urban areas. Some elementary schools grow their own gardens, and some community centers allow people to use small lots for public projects. Boston, San Francisco, and Seattle are three examples of cities where community gardening is popular and successful.

Kids, too, can do many things to help. For example, one possible project is to turn a vacant lot into a community garden that provides fresh food for local people. Kids can ask questions of their elected officials to find out who owns the vacant lot. They can contact the owner of the lot to get permission to build the garden.

If the lot is on public land, attending public hearings and meetings may be required. Participating in community hearings, attending local school board meetings, or getting involved in any civic gathering on important issues can be exciting and empowering. In fact, kids often stand out in a group of adults and therefore have a better chance of attracting support.

The next step might be to create a survey to ask how the neighbors might feel about a garden in their neighborhood. Later on, if the garden is successful, kids can help determine how the food will be distributed. Community gardens are a great way to learn about science, teamwork, and the importance of conservation.

Members of a community garden work together to provide food.

Besides helping create community gardens, kids can bring about change in other ways as well. They can participate in public events such as rallies or demonstrations that raise awareness of hunger and food insecurity. Kids can make posters or signs that express their opinion on issues such as funding for programs that help people get food. The most important thing is to get involved.

Letter Writing

When kids write letters to local, state, or federal officials, they make their voices heard in a powerful way. Sometimes, local officials have fewer than 1,000 **constituents**. A letter from a concerned person can influence a vote and make a difference. One way kids can express their opinions about hunger in the United States is to write letters to officials about the need for food pantries and emergency shelters.

Kids can also write letters about any other subject they feel strongly about. For example, many young people, including Lindsey, care deeply about preserving natural resources. Water, soil, and wood exist on the earth in limited amounts. Working to conserve elements of nature is one way to keep the earth a healthy place for everyone. Taking the time to write a letter to a local, state, or national official shows that kids care enough to want to be part of a solution.

More Ways to Get Involved

Many kids across the country have come up with creative ways to help fight hunger. Some hold canned food drives, volunteer time, and educate people about the problem of food insecurity.

To hold a canned food drive, kids make flyers and posters and hang them in their school or community center. Kids can decorate boxes or bins in which to collect the food. Once the food is collected, it can be given to a food bank or to families in need.

Volunteering is another way to participate in the fight against hunger. For example, students have volunteered to help make sandwiches as a class project. One

Young people take part in a community food drive, collecting packaged foods that can be given to people in need.

group of students can assemble the sandwiches, while others wrap them and take them to a shelter or food bank.

Educating other people about hunger is another way youth across the country are helping those who are less fortunate. Many people think that hunger is not a problem in the United States. Kids can play an important role in letting people know that there are many people in the United States who do not know where they will get their next meal.

Across the world and throughout the country, kids are changing the world for the better. The satisfaction that comes from helping others is a feeling people of all ages can share. In the words of Martin Luther King Jr., "Everybody can be great because anybody can serve. You don't have to have a college degree to serve. You don't have to make your subject and your verb agree to serve. . . . You only need a heart full of grace, a soul generated by love."[17]

Notes

Chapter One: The Early Life of Lindsey Williams

1. Quoted in "Lindsey Williams, Making Her Mark at Central," *Talon*, Winter 2005–2006. www.centralmethodist.edu/alum/ Talon %20Stories/lindsey.html.

2. Quoted in "Missouri's Top Two Youth Volunteers Selected in 10th Annual National Awards Program," *PR Newswire*, February 9, 2005. www.infozine.com/news/stories/op/ storiesView/sid/5767/.

3. Quoted in "Missouri's Top Two Youth Volunteers Selected in 10th Annual National Awards Program."

Chapter Two: Scientific Experiments

4. Quoted in girlshealth.gov, "Spotlight: Lindsey Williams," U.S. Department of Health and Human Services, National Women's Health Information Center (NWHIC), March 2007. www.girlshealth.gov/spot light/2007.03.htm.

5. Quoted in girlshealth.gov, "Spotlight: Lindsey Williams."

6. Quoted in Bruce Gellerman, "Planting Sideways," interview with Lindsey Williams, Living on Earth. www.loe.org/shows/shows. htm?programID=05-P13-00044.

7. Quoted in Gellerman, "Planting Sideways."

Chapter Three: Service and Recognition

8. Quoted in girlshealth.gov, "Spotlight: Lindsey Williams."
9. Quoted in Gellerman, "Planting Sideways."
10. Quoted in Gellerman, "Planting Sideways."
11. Quoted in Tim Engle, "This College Freshman Is Definitely on a Roll," *Kansas City Star*, October 16, 2005, p. 113.

Chapter Four: Tools for the Future

12. Quoted in "Lindsey Williams, Making Her Mark at Central."
13. Quoted in Engle, "This College Freshman Is Definitely on a Roll."
14. Quoted in girlshealth.gov, "Spotlight: Lindsey Williams."
15. Quoted in girlshealth.gov, "Spotlight: Lindsey Williams."

Chapter Five: Ways to Help

16. Quoted in girlshealth.gov, "Spotlight: Lindsey Williams."
17. Martin Luther King Jr., "The Drum Major Instinct," speech delivered at Ebenezer Baptist Church, Atlanta, Georgia, February 4, 1968. www.stanford.edu/group/King/publications/inventory/abbrev.htm#MLKEC.

Glossary

accessibility: The ability to reach or use things.

agricultural engineering: The use of math and science to cultivate soil and grow crops.

conservation: Preservation and restoration of natural resources.

constituents: People who are represented by elected officials.

displacing: The removal of something or someone from its place or position.

drought: A long span of abnormally dry weather that causes damage to living conditions.

innovations: Things that are new or different.

levees: Ridges or raised areas bordering fields built to hold back water.

philanthropy: Actions taken with the intention of benefiting human beings.

submerged: Covered with water.

technology: Science that is used for business or everyday purposes.

For Further Exploration

Books

L. Patricia Kite, *Gardening Wizardry for Kids.* Hauppauge, New York: Barron's Educational Series, 1995. In addition to a large collection of gardening projects, resources, and ideas, this book is also enriched with fun, fascinating history and folklore.

Simon Mugford, *My Big Science Book.* New York: St. Martin's, 2003. Filled with step-by-step instructions for interesting science experiments, this work also features helpful colorful photographs and illustrations.

Felder Rushing, *Dig, Plant, Grow: A Kid's Guide to Gardening.* Nashville, Tennessee: Cool Springs, 2004. This book contains gardening projects, nature facts, and information about ecology.

Web Sites

Feeding Minds, Fighting Hunger (www.feeding minds.org/yw). This Web site, sponsored by the Food and Agriculture Organization of the United Nations, is part of an international effort to get kids involved in the fight against world hunger. The link titled "Youth Window" opens a wide variety of resources available for kids who want to become involved.

Girls Science Center and Girls Only (http://plugged-in.org/Trans_clubhouse.html, www.gogirlsonly.org/whats up/). These Web sites, hosted by the Girl Scouts of America, provide a variety of resources for girls interested in science and math, as well as girls who want to get involved in volunteering.

Just for Kids (www.urbanext.uiuc.edu/kids/index.html). This Web site, created by the University of Illinois Extension Urban Programs Resource Network, features interactive programs on topics such as "my first garden" and ecology.

Kids Can Make a Difference (www.kidscanmakeadifference.org). The link "What Kids Can Do" leads to a collection of information about ways in which kids can become involved in community action.

Kids Do Ecology Program (www.nceas.ucsb.edu/nceasweb/kids). This organization is dedicated to assisting kids who want to learn more about ecology and environmental issues.

Index

Picture Credits

About the Author

Michelle E. Houle received her Bachelor of Arts from the University of California, San Diego. She lives in San Diego, where she works as a freelance writer. She also teaches at Lindsay Community School, a high school for pregnant and parenting young women in downtown San Diego. She spends her free time listening to music, volunteering, drawing comics, and playing with her two cats.